First Edition, "The Enema Handbook" 2005

Second Edition, "The Complete Enema in April 2006 by Alternative Therapies

ISBN 10: 0-9552887-0-3 ISBN 13: 978-0-9552887-0-8

http://www.therapies.com/ patrick@therapies.com

Disclaimer

The content of this book is for information only.

The author of this book is not a physician, and the ideas, procedures and suggestions in this book are not intended to replace the medical and legal advice of trained professionals. All matters regarding your health require medical supervision. Consult your medical practitioner about any condition that may require diagnosis or medical attention.

The author and publishers cannot he held responsible for any errors and omissions that may be found in the text or any actions that may be taken by a reader as a result of any reliance on the information contained in the txt, which is take entirely at the reader's own risk.

TABLE OF CONTENTS

ENEMAS

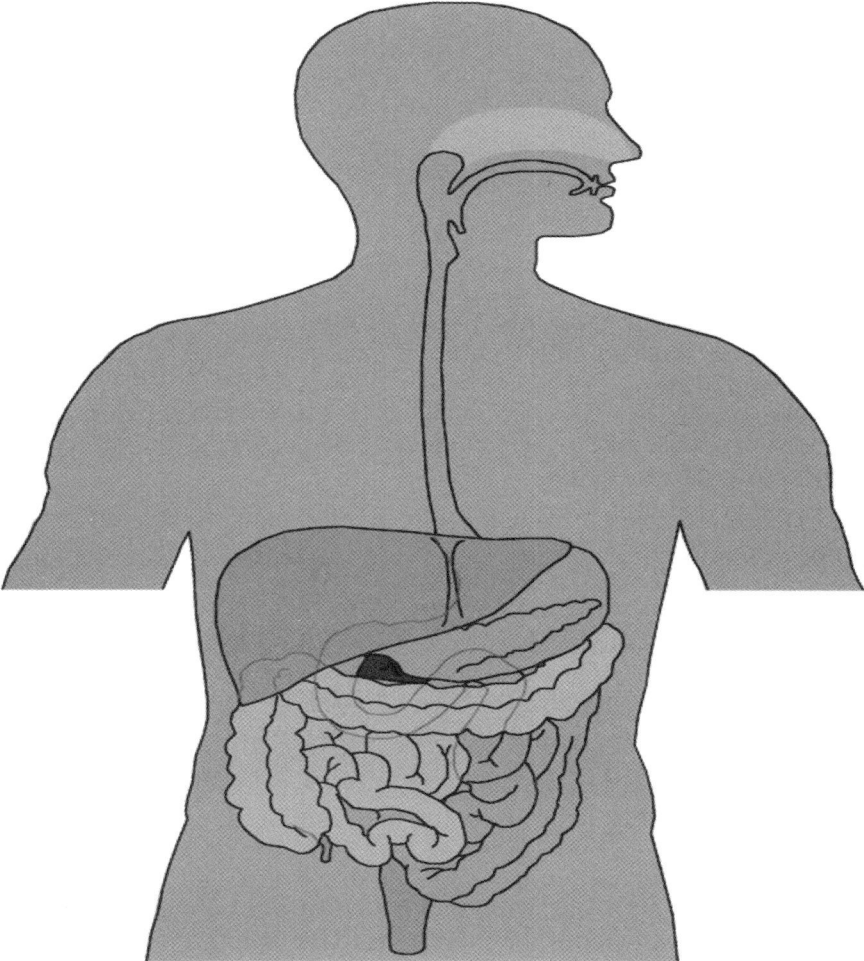

"It is difficult to describe the incredulous facial expressions which ripple across a medical school lecture audience as the topic of enemas is introduced. Embarrassed sniggering is heard from several seats in the hall.

A wise guy heckles "How do you take it?"

Charlotte Gerson doesn't miss a beat, answering: "Black - without cream or sugar"

Laughter relaxes the entire room and Charlotte goes on to explain this aspect of her famous father's treatment (Max Gerson MD).

(Excerpted from "The Little Enema Book" - for those on the Gerson Therapy)

What are enemas?

An enema consist of a fluid injected in the anus to clear out the rectum /sigmoid colon and possibly some of the descending colon or for injecting food or drugs.

The history of enemas

The word enema comes from the Greek en-hienai, translated as "to inject or to send into".

The oldest reference to enemas come from the Ebers Papyrus dated 1,500 BC.

Thousands of years prior to this text, the Pharaoh had 'a guardian of the anus' in the person of a doctor whose duty was the administration of the Royal enema.

Enemas have probably been used for tens/ hundreds of thousands or millions of years.

American Indians used an animal bladder to hold the liquid and a hollow leg bone to dispense the mixture into the anus.

South Americans (pre Columbians) shaped latex to create the first enema kits.

In France, prior to the French revolution of 1789, the "after dinner" enema was common. It was said not only to help with a good complexion but also to help maintain health. French King Louis XIV who died in 1715 at the right old age of 77 is said to have taken over 2,000 enemas in his lifetime.

Animals have been known to use enemas. Birds were observed to fill up their beaks with water, then blow the water into their rectum and expel the water. Clever!

In the Gospel of peace of Jesus by the disciple John:

"Seek therefore, a large trailing gourd, take out its inwards and fill it with water from the river which the sun has warmed; hang it upon a branch of a tree and kneel upon the ground before the angel of water and suffer the end of the stalk to enter your hinder parts, that the water may flow through all your bowels. Afterwards, rest kneeling on the ground before the angel of water that he will free your body from every uncleanness and disease."

What are enemas used for?

As previously mentioned, Enemas are used to (partially) remove faeces from the rectum, sigmoid and, to some extent, from the descending colon. They help discharge parasites and get rid of drug residue.

Skin conditions can sometimes be bettered after a series of enemas. Patients with headaches and migraines may also benefit.

The Gerson therapy claims that by detoxifying the liver, a coffee enema can help with cancer (see coffee enemas on page 13)

What reactions can be expected?

As the body detoxifies, the patient may feel a relief from depression and feel more relaxed. Allergy related symptoms may disappear, pain may subside.

As part of a healing crisis, the patient may suffer increased flatulence and gas. In some rare cases, some of the bile may go up in the stomach, through the pyloric sphincter, and cause some nausea. Vomiting may occur. If this happens, it is important to frequently drink copious amounts of peppermint tea to excrete the bile from the stomach. Some Reiki or other healing over the sensitive area will also help.

When a healing crisis occurs, it is a sign that the liver is detoxifying and the frequency of the enemas should be increased. If in doubt as to what to do, consult a qualified therapist.

Is it safe?

Prior to using an enema, you should first consult a metabolic therapist to make sure that there are no intestinal blockages or contra-indications.

Enemas are used in most "Alternative Therapy" clinics in the United States and Mexico. Coffee enemas are, arguably, the best way to detoxify the liver without the harmful use of strong chemicals. The Gerson therapy makes extensive use of enemas, recommending that they should be administered every four hours or more in certain cases.

A qualified therapist should always be consulted for advice when a patient has had chemotherapy treatment or colostomy.

The different positions

There are many positions that can be used when receiving an enema. Three of them are illustrated below:

1 Lying on the right side

Lying on your right side, knees bent up. This position is used for coffee and other enemas when it is important to let the mixture flow up the haemorrhoidal and hepatic portal vein to the liver. This is my preferred position for most enemas.

2 Lying on the left side

Lying on the left hand side. A variation on the above but this does not allow a good flow back to the liver.

3 Head down and backside up

Head down and backside up. Is a good position (although not as relaxing) for most enemas except those where a flow to the liver is recommended.

What should you do during an Enema Cleanse?

Drink more water. It is essential for everyone to drink at least 6 to 8 glasses of water every day. Dehydration is a major cause of constipation and bowel problems. You don't have to be thirsty to be dehydrated. Water is needed to CLEAN OUT TOXINS.

How often can you take an enema?

It is important to know that enemas do not weaken the intestines but strengthens them. They will encourage the peristaltic movement (movement of food in the intestines).

In some Natural cure hospitals,, enemas are recommended several times a day on a daily basis.

However, if you are healthy an enema can be safely taken once or twice a week without problem. If in doubt as to how often you can take an enema, please consult your therapist.

The equipment needed to receive an enema

(You can purchase enema kits from www.therapies.com/acatalog)

I would recommend a 1 litre enema bucket to start with and this is what the following recipes are based on. Once used to enemas, you may want to use a 2 litre bucket.

At the beginning, and sometimes unexpectedly, an enema can be messy and unattractively redecorate your room. It is therefore important to be prepared for the unexpected.

A waterproof, floor or covering of some type should be used to lie on. This can in turn be covered with an old blanket or towel.

Comfort is important, as the treatment will last about 15 to 20 minutes. During the enema, you may read, watch TV, listen to the radio or do whatever you believe you can do with a tube sticking out of your bottom.

Special equipment as follows is needed:

- A waterproof covering or surface
- A blanket or other covering for warmth
- A pillow to support your head
- A roll of absorbent tissues for spillage or to clean up waste
- Vaseline or KY Jelly to lubricate the end of the tube
- A special enema bucket with a tube outlet
- A catheter tube for insertion in the anus
- A fine mesh sieve for the coffee enema
- A platform on which to rest the bucket. This should be about 40 to 50 centimetres higher than the patient but not much more
- A stainless steel pan to heat the water
- A watch to keep track of time

Just before receiving an enema, the patient should eat a small piece of fruit to kick-start the upper part of the digestive process.

The process
- In a clean enema bucket, add the "Enema mixture" (the mixture is the enema recipe)
- Make sure the mixture is at body temperature (100-102 Fahrenheit or 37-38 Celsius)
- Open the tube and run a little bit of the liquid to get rid of the residual air. Close the tube again
- Go to the place where you are going to receive the enema

11

- Place the bucket 40-50 cms above you
- Lubricate the end of the catheter tube with some Vaseline or KY jelly.
- For coffee enemas It is best to lie on your **right** side to help the absorption of the enema mixture through the haemorrhoidal and portal veins. However, it is also fine to lie on the left side or on your front, whatever position you feel comfortable (see positions on page 8).
- Slightly bend your knees towards your abdomen
- Insert about 5 to 8 cms of the tube into your rectum (it is important not to insert too much of the tube as otherwise you may damage the fine membranes in your rectum or sigmoid colon)
- Open the tube and let the "enema mixture" flow in
- Keep the tube open and connected to the bucket during the treatment. Whilst the mixture is in your intestines, you may feel some pressure and gas. An open tube will allow this pressure to be released.
- The bucket should empty in about 2-3 minutes.
- Retain the enema for a further 15 - 20 minutes.
- Go to the toilet and excrete the mixture
- Keep your equipment clean. Wash it after each use with a good biodegradable product such as Ecover washing up liquid. Use a 6% hydrogen peroxide solution to thoroughly clean the equipment.

It is a good idea when receiving the enema to massage your abdomen in a counter clockwise motion. This will help the enema mixture to move higher up into the colon.

When expelling the enema, it is a good idea to massage your abdomen in a clockwise motion to help the mixture come out of your colon. Bringing your knees up and squatting when expelling the enema will also help.

The different types of enemas

In the following recipes, I have assumed you are using a one-litre (1 quart) enema bucket. Should you be using a two-litre enema bucket, then you obviously need to double the amount of water.

1- Coffee Enemas

The history of Coffee enemas

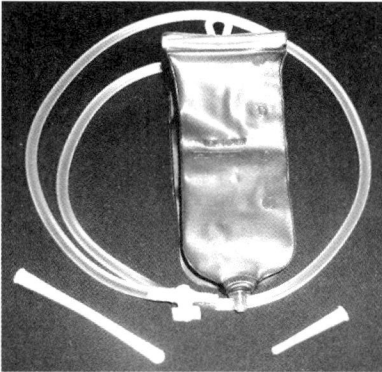

Coffee enemas were discovered, during the First World War by German nurses trying to help soldier with their pains.

Many of the soldiers receiving treatment for their wounds were also prescribed water enemas for their constipation.

Nurses had observed that doctors were able to keep awake and perform their duties for much longer when they drank coffee. The nurses had a plentiful supply of coffee and decided to use some of it in the enemas. Often, soldiers reported that their pains lessened or disappeared after the coffee enemas and their health improved.

A couple of German professors were intrigued by this discovery and decided to investigate further. They found out that the caffeine entered the liver via the haemorrhoidal veins and subsequently the hepatic portal veins. The caffeine caused an increase in the flow of bile that allowed toxins to be released and excreted from the body.

Apart from the by products of the food we eat, poisons and toxins we store in our body include medicines, HRT, oral contraceptives, mercury from tooth fillings, fluoride from water supplies,

13

pesticides, weed killers, plasticisers and numerous other synthetic chemicals. Our tap water may contain the residues of other peoples' medicines and synthetic hormones, so just because we eat a clean diet and take no drugs, doesn't mean that we are not absorbing these types of toxins.

Our liver is the organ in charge of the detoxification process.

Disease eventually occurs when our body is overloaded with these toxins or when emotional trauma(s) undermine our immune system (see Emotional Freedom Therapy to find a tool to deal with this and read "The EFT Coach" for recommended reading).

Research carried out in 1981 by Dr Lee Wattenberg and colleagues showed that the 'kahweol' and 'cafestol palmitate' found in coffee encouraged the activity of the enzyme 'glutathione S-transferase'. This enzyme neutralises free radicals and harmful chemicals often linked with the beginning of cancer. The dilation to the bile ducts caused by the coffee enemas are believed to be a contributor to carcinogen detoxification by the liver.

Furthermore, theophylline and theobromine (two other chemicals in coffee) dilate blood vessels and heals the inflammation of the colon.

What is the Coffee enema for?

- Detoxifies the liver/gallbladder
- It opens the bile ducts
- Produces enzyme activity for oxygen uptake and helps the formation of red blood cells
- To some extent flushes deposits from the large intestines
- Increases the movement of food through the intestines (peristaltic movement)
- Stimulates the digestive tracts

- Believed by Dr Max Gerson (of the Gerson therapy) that by detoxifying the liver and gall bladder, coffee enemas could help the health of cancer patients.
- Releases toxins and helps control pain

Recipe

- In a clean stainless steel saucepan, boil 1 litre (about 1 quart) of distilled or filtered water
- Gradually add 3 level tablespoons of the best organic ground coffee you can buy.
- Boil for 5 further minutes uncovered
- Cover and simmer for 15 minutes.
- Turn off the heat
- Sieve the mixture in the enema bucket (making sure the tube coming off it is closed).
- The enema will be ready to use when the temperature goes down to body temperature (100-102 Fahrenheit or 37-38 Celsius)
- Refer to "The process" on page 11 for instructions on what to do during the enema
- Make sure to breathe deeply during the whole treatment to help the absorption of coffee

Note: Nowadays, I only boil half the water I need for the coffee enema and top it up with cold filtered water. This saves me some of the "cooling down time".

If your intestines are not able to absorb the whole litre the first few times, this is not a problem. Just keep doing it. Eventually, your body will take it. I personally often use a 2-litre enema bucket.

Above all, I recommend that you consult a practitioner who is familiar with coffee enema techniques and can guide you through any potential hazard you may come across.

Notes

Coffee enemas are best taken in the morning.

Coffee enemas can be very dehydrating, so make sure you drink plenty of water

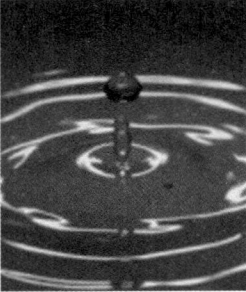

2- Water Enema

A most gentle enema

What for?

- Cleanses the rectum and sigmoid colon
- Rehydrates the colon and the body

Recipe

- The mixture should consist of approximately 1 litre (1 quart) of body temperature (100-102 Fahrenheit or 37-38 Celsius) water
- Follow "The process" - see page 11

3- Garlic Enema

What for?

- Cleanses the liver and the intestines of mucous congestion
- Combats cholesterol
- Clears harmful bacteria and parasites
- Gets rid of worms
- A great natural antiseptic
- Useful for yeast infection.

Recipe

- Crush 2 to 3 cloves of garlic in a half litre (1/2 quart) of water and bring to the boil.
- Simmer the mixture for 10 minutes.
- Add about ½ litre (half a quart) of filtered cold water so the enema mixture reaches body temperature (100-102 Fahrenheit or 37-38 Celsius)
- Follow "The process" - see page 11

4- Red Raspberry enemas

What for?

- Assist reproductive system
- Good potassium, magnesium, zinc, silica and iron content

Recipe

- 2 tablespoons to ½ litre (1/2 quart) of water
- Bring the water to the boil
- Let simmer for 15 minutes
- Top up the mixture with cold filtered water to bring the mixture to body temperature (100-102 Fahrenheit or 37-38 Celsius) to a quantity of approximately 1 litre
- Follow "The process" – see page 11

5- Epsom Salt Enema

What for?

- Soothe and calms the colon
- Has a laxative effect
- Increases the amount of water in the intestines, producing a bowel movement

Recipe

- Mix 2 tablespoons of Epsom salt to 1 litre of body temperature (100-102 Fahrenheit or 37-38 Celsius) water
- Follow "The process" – see page 11

6- Garlic/Epsom Salt Enema

What for?

- Very purging

Recipe

- 2 cloves of pressed garlic to 1 litre of "body temperature (100-102 Fahrenheit or 37-38 Celsius)" water
- Bring to the boil and simmer for 10 minutes
- Add 2 tablespoon of Epsom Salt and mix thoroughly
- Follow "The process" - see page 11

7- Castile Soap Enema

Castile soap is made with Coconut or Olive oil (Castile is sometimes spelt Castille)

It is advisable to follow this enema with a water enema to flush all soap and prevent any irritation.

What for?

- Gently cleanses the colon
- Helps relieve stubborn constipation

Recipe

- Use 5 mls (0.17 US ounce) of Castille soap to 1 litre (1 quart) of water to your enema. Make sure the Castille soap is fully dissolved in the water.
- Follow the instructions in "The process" on page 11

8- Salt Water Enema

This is the most often used enema in hospitals.

What for?

- Relieve constipation
- Cleanses the bowels
- Reduces the amount of water in and out of the colon and prevents too much urination afterwards

Recipe

- Add 1 level tablespoon of fine sea salt to 1 litre of "body temperature (100-102 Fahrenheit or 37-38 Celsius)" water
- Follow "The process" – see page 11

9- Fennel Enema

What for?

- Calms the nervous system
- Relieves gas
- Helps get rid of worms
- Detoxifying
- Stimulates digestion

Recipe

- 2 tablespoons of fennel to ½ litre (1/2 quart) of water
- Bring the water to the boil

19

- Let simmer for 15 minutes
- Top up the mixture with cold filtered water to bring the mixture to body temperature (100-102 Fahrenheit or 37-38 Celsius) to a quantity of approximately 1 litre
- Follow "The process" – see page 11

10- Wheatgrass Enema

What for?

- Stimulates and cleanses the liver (in the same way as for a Coffee enema, the mixture is absorbed through the haemorrhoidal vein, into the hepatic portal vein and into the gallbladder and liver)
- Wheatgrass will add oxygen to the whole body
- It will increase your energy level
- The wheatgrass will increase the peristaltic action of the colon
- It helps get rid of old faeces

Recipe

- Use a juicer to juice 120 grams (about 4 ounces) of wheatgrass
- Add the juice to one litre (1 quart) of body temperature (100-102 Fahrenheit or 37-38 Celsius)) water.
- Follow "The process" – see page 11

11- Catnip Enema

What for?

- To reduce a fever and keep it down
- To soothe and relax the intestines
- Relieves gas

- To rehydrate the body
- To help with constipation or diarrhoea
- Good for stomach and digestive disorders
- Removes toxins and unfriendly bacteria from the intestines

Recipe

- Bring 1 litre (1 quart) of filtered water to the boil
- If you can get fresh dried catnip leaves, use 8 tablespoons otherwise if you are using tea bags, use whatever is recommended for 1 litre of water
- Pour the water over the catnip tea
- Let the mixture rest for about 10 minutes
- Strain the mixture
- Add some cold filtered water
- When at body temperature (100-102 Fahrenheit or 37-38 Celsius),
- Follow "The process" – see page 11

12- Chamomile Tea Enema

Chamomile is sometimes spelt Camomille

What for?

- Can help haemorrhoids
- Gently soothes and cleanses the colon
- Gently cleanses the liver
- Help relieve nausea
- Promotes relaxation

Recipe

- Boil 1 litre of water
- Add 3 tea bags to the water

- Let it steep for 5-10 minutes
- Remove the tea bags
- Add cold filtered water so the mixture reaches body temperature (100-102 Fahrenheit or 37-38 Celsius)
- Follow "The process" – see page 11

13- Magnesium Citrate Enema

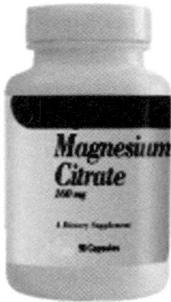

What for?

- Cleanses
- Relaxes
- Rehydrates
- Alkalise the blood

Recipe

- Add two capsules of magnesium citrate to 1 litre of body temperature (100-102 Fahrenheit or 37-38 Celsius) water
- Follow "The process" – see page 11 ###

14- Ginger Enema

What for?

- Soothing
- Anti-inflammatory
- Good to clear congestion
- Supports the liver
- Helps clear headaches
- Good for circulation
- Helps to disperse gas

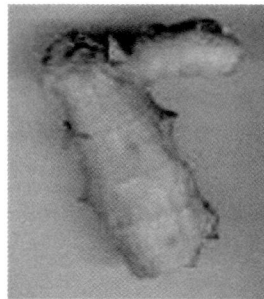

Recipe

- Grate a golf ball size piece of ginger
- Squeeze the juice out into a bowl
- Prepare 1 litre of body temperature (100-102 Fahrenheit or 37-38 Celsius) water
- Pour the ginger juice into the water using a sieve to filter out the bits
- Follow "The process" – see page 11

Note

Make sure you do not boil the ginger, as it would lose its property

15- Burdock Enema

What for?

- Good for the kidneys and bladder
- Good for the skin
- Good for the hair
- Great for the blood
- Breaks down calcium deposits

Recipe

- 2 tablespoons to ½ litre (1/2 quart) of water
- Bring the water to the boil
- Let simmer for 15 minutes
- Top up the mixture with cold filtered water to bring the mixture to body temperature (100-102 Fahrenheit or 37-38 Celsius) to a quantity of approximately 1 litre
- Follow "The process" – see page 11

16- Castor Oil Enema

What for?
- Helps cleanse the bowels
- Stimulates the liver

Recipe
- Add ¼ litre (1/4 quart) of linseed oil to ¾ litre (3/4 quart) of body temperature (100-102 Fahrenheit or 37-38 Celsius) water
- Follow "The process" – see page 11

17- Linseed Oil Enema

What for?
- Anti-inflammatory
- Releases sodium from the cells
- Promotes cellular activity
- Promotes liver and bowel functions

Recipe
- Add ¼ litre (1/4 quart) of linseed oil to 3/4 litre (3/4 quart) of body temperature (100-102 Fahrenheit or 37-38 Celsius) water
- Follow "The process" – see page 11

Notes
This is best done in the evening before bedtime. Be careful... wear some form of padding in your underwear (you have been warned).

18- Green Tea Enema

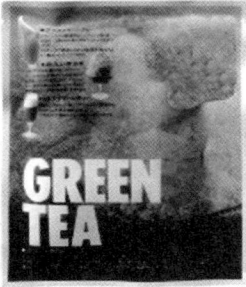

This contains a powerful antioxidant: polyphenol oxidase

(you would have to eat more than 21 fruits and vegetable to get this amount of antioxidant from your food)

Your body naturally produces chemicals called free radicals that cause irreversible damage (oxidation) to cells. They can leave your body vulnerable to advanced aging, cancer, cardiovascular disease, and degenerative diseases like arthritis, pancreatic and prostate problems.

Antioxidants are necessary to combat this degenerative process as they combat oxidation.

What for?
- To release antioxidants into the bloodstream
- Helps replenish the good bacteria in your large intestines
- May help IBS (Irritable Bowel Syndrome) and Colitis

Recipe
- Boil 1/2 litre (1/2 quart) of filtered water
- Just before boiling point, add 2 tablespoon of green tea leaves
- Cover and allow to brew for 4-5 minutes
- Strain the mixture
- Allow to cool to body temperature by adding some cold filtered water (100-102 Fahrenheit or 37-38 Celsius) and enjoy

19- Spirulina Enema

What for?
- Helps detoxify both blood and bowels

Recipe

- 2 tablespoons of Spirulina powder to 1litre of water
- follow "The process" – see page 11

20- Aloe Vera Enema

What for?

- Good for haemorrhoids
- Anti-inflammatory
- Promotes the right ph balance within the bowels
- Assists in the production of friendly bacteria to the intestines
- Will help irritable bowel and diverticulitis
- Cleanses the colon well
- If some olive oil is added to the mixture, it will soothe the intestinal track

Recipe

- Boil 1/2 litre (1/2 quart) of filtered water
- Add 4-5 tablespoons of Aloe Vera to the water
- Add cold filtered water to make up one litre
- When the mixture is at body temperature (100-102 Fahrenheit or 37-38 Celsius),
- Follow "The process" – see page 11

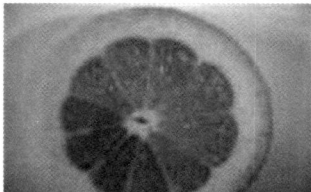

21- Lemon Juice Enema

Lemon is a mild irritant that may increase intestinal cramps during the process

What for?

- To help cleanse your colon of old faeces

- Helps balance the ph factor in the blood

Recipe
- Bring about ½ litre (1/2 quart) of filtered water to the boil
- Add the juice of 1to 2 lemons (about 1/3rd of a cup)
- Add ½ litre (1/2 quart) of cold filtered water
- When the mixture is at body temperature (100-102 Fahrenheit or 37-38 Celsius), follow "The process" – see page 11

22- Urine Enema
OK.. lets deal with the objections first:

Urine is a waste product

A **misconception**: Your urine is the result of the filtration of your blood by the kidneys. If you urine is of bad quality, this means that your blood is also of bad quality. In which case, you should seriously start thinking about changing your diet and lifestyle. If your diet is good and your blood is of good quality, then your urine will contain whatever surplus your body does not need at present. Many nutrients such as:

- Hormones (aldosterone, androgens, androsterone, estradiol, estriol, estrone etc..)
- Many minerals such as magnesium, manganese, iron, calcium, zinc etc..
  Inositol, glycine, iodine, alanine, ascorbic acid, biotin, cystine, dopamine, folic acid, potassium can also be found
- Vitamin B6, B12
- Enzymes, co enzymes

and many more essential ingredients are contained in your urine. It also is in a form that is readily absorbable by the body as it has already been digested.

But surely there must be some toxins in my urine?

OK, nobody is perfect. Because of your diet and lifestyle, it is granted that some toxins will find their way into your urine. But even those are beneficial.

You may have heard about homeopathy. In homeopathy, a patient is given a small dose of a poison that would cause similar symptoms to the ones he is suffering from. The body will recognise the poison and react against it and fight the disease.

We have the same process with urine. By re-ingesting a minute dose of your own poison, you are going to force the body to fight against something it does not like. So, as we can see, even if some toxins are present in your urine, it is also beneficial.

Convinced? - please don't let your education and left brain prevent you from using this wonderful remedy. It is free and one of the most effective remedies I have ever found.

What for?

- To help cleanse your colon
- A good supply of vitamins, minerals, enzyme etc..
- Regenerates intestinal flora

Recipe

- Use a 50/50 mixture of urine and water
- Make sure the mixture is at room temperature
- Follow "The process" – see page 11

Castor oil pack

I have included this recipe in this book as this is one of the best methods to flush toxins out of the body.

Castor oil packs were often mentioned by Edgar Cayce.

The following has been reproduced from http://www.edgarcayce.org/Edgar-Cayce.html

"For forty-three years of his adult life, Edgar Cayce demonstrated the uncanny ability to put himself into some kind of self-induced sleep state by lying down on a couch, closing his eyes, and folding his hands over his stomach. This state of relaxation and meditation enabled him to place his mind in contact with all time and space. From this state he could respond to questions as diverse as, "What are the secrets of the universe?" to "How can I remove a wart?" His responses to these questions came to be called "readings" and contain insights so valuable that even to this day individuals have found practical help for everything from maintaining a well-balanced diet and improving human relationships to overcoming life-threatening illnesses and experiencing a closer walk with God.

From:
http://www.arebookstore.com/product.asp?pn=568&sid=INTEC

Castor oil has a long history of traditional medical use dating back to ancient Egypt. Derived from the castor bean (Ricinus communis), the oil was once used internally as a laxative but is now primarily used externally due to its potential toxicity."

What for?

The pack is placed onto the skin to increase circulation, promote elimination of toxins and speed up the healing of tissues and organs. It stimulates the liver, increases lymphatic circulation, relieves pain, improves digestion and reduces inflammation.

Recipe

You may lie down or sit comfortably in a recliner armchair for this treatment

- Lay plastic (bin liners are fine) on the bed or armchair you are going to use for the treatment
- Soak a thick cotton flannel in castor oil (double it if necessary)
- Squeeze the excess castor oil out of the flannel
- Place the flannel directly in contact with the skin
- Cover the flannel with a plastic sheet
- Place a heating pad (preferred) or a hot water bottle on top of the plastic
- Wrap yourself in a blanket for warmth
- Enjoy the next hour reading a book/ watching TV/ listening to your favourite CDs etc..
- It is best not to move when using a Castor oil pack although possible

After removing the pack, cleanse the skin with a dilute solution of water and baking soda. I also often scrub my skin with kitchen towels before entering the shower (not orthodox but it works!)

Store the pack in a covered container in the refrigerator. Each pack may be reused up to 25-30 times.

A castor oil pack can be placed on the following body regions:

- The right side of the abdomen to stimulate the liver. Castor oil packs are often recommended as part of a liver detox program.
- Inflamed and swollen joints, bursitis, and muscle strains.
- The abdomen to relieve constipation and other digestive disorders.
- The lower abdomen in cases of menstrual irregularities and uterine and ovarian cysts.

Safety precautions

Castor oil should not be taken internally.

It should not be applied to broken skin, or used during pregnancy, breastfeeding, or during menstrual flow.

Frequency of use

It is generally recommended that a castor oil pack be used for 3 to 7 days in a week to treat a health condition or for detox.

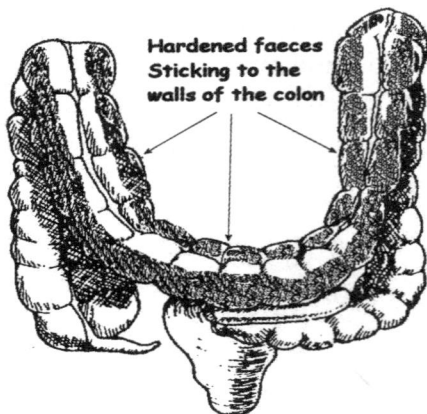

THE COLON

Hardened faeces
Sticking to the
walls of the colon

This booklet would not be complete without an explanation on the importance of keeping your colon clean:

The cleanliness of our colon, in these days of fast food, genetic modifying, pesticides, fertilizers, additives, colouring, preservatives, irradiation, flavouring, high fat intake, sugar etc.. is under a lot of pressure to say the least.

Dr. Bernard Jensen in his book "Tissue Cleansing Through Bowel Management" claimed that over 95% of people he saw in his consultations were constipated. **This may well be your case!**

Although you may have daily bowel movements. Are you sure that 100% of the nutrients your body does not need are coming out? Is it possible that only 99.9% are rejected and the rest sticks to your intestines? What does this mean over a period of 10 or 20 years?

Some health experts say that 90% of all sickness and diseases are related to an unclean colon!

At the beginning of this 21st century, statistics tell us that one person in three will get cancer. More and more people are dying from colon cancer than ever before. It now is the number 1 cancer amongst men and women together. Individually, colon cancer is second only to lung cancer in terms of cancer deaths in the U.S.A.., claiming the lives of nearly 50,000 men and women annually, and yet most people still think "it won't happen to me".

The intestines can store a vast amount of partially digested, putrefying matter (as well as drugs and other toxic chemicals) for decades. The average person stores between **5 to 25 POUNDS** of waste accumulated over the years in their colon. Some intestines, when autopsied, have weighed up to 40 pounds and were distended to a diameter of 12 inches (30 cms) with only a pencil-thin channel through which the faeces could move.

That 40 pounds was due to caked layers of encrusted mucous mixed with faecal matter called a mucoid plaque. This bizarrely resembles hardened blackish-green truck tire rubber (see above picture). Mucoid plaque may vary considerably, depending on the chemical conditions in a person's intestines. It may be hard and brittle; it may be firm and thick; tough, wet, and rubbery; soft, thick, and mucoid; or soft, transparent, and thin; it can range in colour from light brown, black, or greenish-black to yellow or grey, and sometimes emits an intensely foul odour. At 98F degree's temperature (37C), the plaque begins to rot and decay, sending toxins and poisons into the blood stream and throughout the body. Causing endless health problems. Read more information from Dr Richard Anderson at the end of this article.

Waste build up causes bacteria and toxins to spread throughout the body resulting in sickness and even death.

Are you likely to have this mucoid plaque?

If you have had for many years a diet with regular helpings of dairy, deep fried food, hydrogenated fats, coffee or tea, sugar, white flour, microwaved food.

Or if you have had regular toxins or chemicals (in food, at home or outside), heavy metals (including dental mercury), drugs (such as aspirin or alcohol)

Then, you most likely have impacted faecal matter in your colon.

Prolapsed Colon

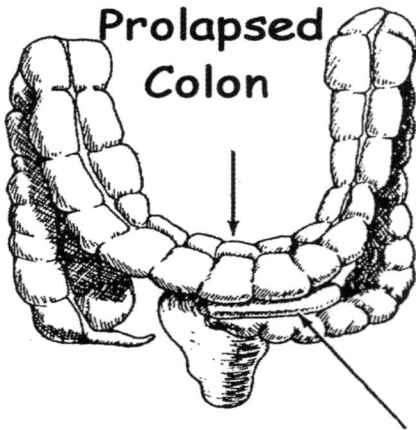

Dr. Richard Schulze believes that some of the methods for colon cleansing don't work any more. This is because our diet is now so far removed from what it should be. Our diet is generally now full of food that has been changed in many ways from what nature intended. Chemicals are added, nutrients and fibres are removed, heating processes change the molecular structure of the food and destroy any life energy. In addition, we now get hardly any exercise, whereas our forebears used to walk everywhere. And then there's the added stress of today's style of living, and electromagnetic stress (from computers, mobile phones, cars, etc.).

Believe it or not, Dr. Richard Schulze and other doctors have had people in their clinic who had only ONE BOWEL MOVEMENT A MONTH! So where did all that food go? These people had their bowels frozen solid. Their other organs were being squashed by all the extra material down there.

Wild animals that are living as nature intended do not get these problems. These problems are not caused by accident. Our living away from nature causes them. You owe it to yourself to LEARN about how you can prevent and even heal these diseases. There is no "one way", no "magic bullet. But there are ways that work. The best methods include nutrition and cleanses. These are the very things that your doctor won't tell you about - because they never learned them. The average doctor learns around 4-20 hours of nutrition during a FIVE-YEAR degree.

In addition to learning about nutrition, many people have had great results from doing an Enema cleanse, of the colon, kidneys and liver. The MOST important cleanse to do is colon cleansing, because if you have a dirty colon with impacted faecal matter, this will create extra toxins which the other organs then have to continually detoxify.

Famous herbalists such as Dr. John Christopher, Dr. Jensen and Paavo Airola, all believed that a major cause of most disease is a dirty bowel. The Merck Manual, the medical industry's standard text for the diagnosis and treatment of disease, tells us that colon degeneration is increasing at an alarming rate. Here are its figures for diverticulosis for people over 45 years old:

- 1950 10%
- 1955 15%
- 1972 30%
- 1987 Almost 50%
- Unknown today but likely to be much higher than in 1987..

What to do?

Since "Death begins in the colon," your nutritional program should begin with a good colon-cleansing program. Toxins and waste build up in your colon just like they do in the pipes of your home. Both demand immediate attention or the results can be disastrous!

Your colon is one of the largest muscles in your body and should be exercised regularly. Of course, physical exercise is beneficial for the colon, but water and fibre is even MORE important. Fibre is a bulking agent that gives the colon the resistance it needs in order to remain firm and active. If the colon is inactive, it will soon grow weak, just like any other muscle. Colon inactivity may hinder the movement of waste material along the intestinal track to be eliminated from the body.

Colon Cleansing promotes Good Health. Gets rid of most of the toxins that are inside your colon that are causing your body not to perform, as it should! I know this is a subject that you don't hear much about. But, what if no one talks about it? More people have problems with their colon than most people realise.

Besides the poisonous effect this has on your body, waste build up hinders the nutrient absorption your body so badly needs. By not eating healthy foods, and not exercising on a regular basis, our system has a tough time digesting foods properly. If your digestive system is not working properly, it also makes it very hard to lose weight because your body's not breaking down and excreting all the food you eat.

For a system to be "regular", it should produce 2-3 bowel movements a day, shortly after each meal.

Internal cleansing is more important than external cleansing and a regular enema can help you.

IMPORTANT POINTS FOR EVERYONE:

The key to maintaining your health is to improve your diet and drink enough water.

Mucoid Plaque by Richard Anderson, N.D., N.M.D.

The trouble is once the mucoid plaque is created, for whatever biologically important reason; it is not routinely excreted from the intestines. Instead it lodges in the numerous folds and crevices of this large organ and can remain there for many years.

Over time, the mucoid plaque grows thicker, firmer, and more widespread colonizing, as it were, the tennis court-sized interior of the intestines. Old faeces adhere to the plaque and are not removed during a normal bowel motion. The plaque slows down intestinal action, both waste excretion and nutrient absorption. It can harbour pathogens, including bacteria and parasites, which actually hide underneath the plaque; it may block the normal outflow of lymph and mucin drainage. It binds toxins to itself and contributes to bowel toxicity, slowly emitting toxins into the bloodstream.

Finally, the plaque creates a friendly environment for disease, in some cases for colon cancer and gastric carcinomas. Gradually your immune system is weakened as the chronically toxic bowel environment destroys useful bacteria. Your liver becomes overburdened by the unprocessed intestinal toxins, and meridian points in the intestines related to hundreds of other parts of the body are compromised. A toxic bowel results in toxic blood and lymph, toxic organs and cells, and toxic function. The bowel "feeds" every organ, tissue, and cell in our bodies, so when the quality of feeding from the digestive system is contaminated or of poor quality, the cells and organs elsewhere in the body will be compromised and grow sluggish and inefficient. So while mucoid plaque is "natural" in that the intestines produce it, it is most unnatural in that the presence of a large amount of it indicates a high degree of intestinal ill health. When the intestines are ill, you will be ill.

Herbal Colon Cleanse

What to do if you have suffered from constipation for years?

Should your colon be in a bad state, I would strongly recommend that you do a herbal colon cleanse. You may discontinue the enemas whilst doing the colon cleanse.

Ideally, your colon cleanse should consist of 3 natural herbal ingredients:

1. Activated charcoal
2. Intestinal Tone
3. Herbal tabs

This can be ordered from http://www.therapies.com

Activated Charcoal

This is a natural deodorant and disinfectant.

Made by heating coconut shells in the absence of air, partly-burned shells are granulated to a size that provides for optimum absorption. This vegetable form of carbon (an element found in all living matter), is completely safe for human consumption.

It is one of the finest natural absorbent agents known and recognized by the FDA, and has been used by physicians and natural healers throughout the world for centuries. It is particularly helpful in providing relief for trapped gas in the lower intestine; physicians and regulatory agencies also acknowledge charcoal's cleansing and healing properties. Known as the universal antidote, charcoal is used in hospital emergency rooms to neutralize drugs and poisons. It also makes a great addition to any family first aid kit.

Many years of research have proven that activated charcoal is safe, very effective and free of dangerous side effects. It has the amazing ability to attract itself to, and absorb, thousands of times its own weight in gases, heavy metals, toxins, poisons and other chemicals, thus making them ineffective or harmless. Activated charcoal is without rival as an agent for cleansing and assisting the healing processes of the body, and orally administered activated charcoal has proven to be very effective in preventing many intestinal infections.

The granular form of activated charcoal was chosen as part of its Colon Cleanse Program because in that form it has a very high rate of adsorption. Once toxins and gases are adsorbed by the charcoal they are not released back into the system but rather are held by the charcoal until eliminated from the body.

It is of interest to note that even today the mechanism by which charcoal works, either from a physical or chemical standpoint, it is not completely known. However, research shows that it has the ability to distinguish toxins from nutrients and will not adsorb nutrients.

Herbal Tabs

This stimulating herbal tonic is both cleansing, healing and strengthening to the entire gastro-intestinal system. It stimulates the muscular movement of the colon and over time strengthens the muscles of the large intestine, halts putrefaction and disinfects, soothes and heals the mucous membrane lining of your entire digestive tract.

It improves digestion, relieves gas and cramps, increases the flow of bile which in turn cleans the gall bladder, bile ducts and liver, helps destroy CANDIDA ALBICANS overgrowth, promotes a healthy intestinal flora, destroys and expels intestinal parasites, increases gastrointestinal circulation. It's anti-bacterial, anti-viral and anti-fungal.

This formula synergistically combines health-enhancing herbs and sea vegetation that nourishes and cleanses the bowels while aiding healthy elimination.

Herbal Tab's mild, natural and non-habit forming phytonutrients break down impacted accumulation along colon walls and flush out the accumulated toxins that the Detoxifying Charcoal has been collecting.. They are mild, natural and non-habit forming.

It is recommended, while on this program, to drink 6-8 glasses of water daily.

INGREDIENTS:

- SENNA - an excellent source of cathartic acid that fosters safe and brisk elimination.
- BUCKTHORN BARK - A mild, but certain purgative found useful in habitual constipation.

41

- PEPPERMINT - A soothing anti-spasmodic which alleviates discomfort, reduces flatulency
- LICORICE ROOT - A popular flavouring agent which reduces cramping while facilitating the effects of other herbs.
- CASCARA SAGRADA - A natural bark that is the most widely used cathartic on earth.
- PSYLLIUM HUSKS - An effective bulking agent.
- FENNEL SEED - A common flavouring agent that expels gas and relieves colic.
- CITRUS PEEL POWDER - An unexpected source of relief for colic
- GINGER - A well-known spice that relieves cramping and colic while stimulating the mucous membrane.
- PEPSIN - A natural enzyme that breaks down proteins.
- RHUBARB ROOT - A natural blood cleanser used for chronic indigestion.
- ANIS SEED - A long-used spice that expels gas.
- BLUE MALVA FLOWER - A beautiful flower with mild laxative properties.

SEA VEGETATION - a blend of sea vegetation that detoxifies the bowels while providing an exceptional source of vitamins, macro minerals, ultra trace minerals, enzymes and amino acids.

Intestinal Tone

Intestinal Tone is a natural blend of psyllium husks and psyllium seeds that provides the optimal mix of soluble and insoluble fibres (80% husk and 20% seed).

Both gentle and effective, the soluble fibre from the husks helps absorb and eliminate cholesterol, fats and toxins that accumulate in the colon. The insoluble fibre from the seeds provides the bulk needed to promote peristaltic action and eliminate waste while allowing for improved absorption of nutrients.

Intestinal Tone contains no chemical stimulants, sugar, salt, preservatives or artificial flavours. This is a fibre product. Low fat diets rich in fibre-containing grain products, fruits, and vegetables may reduce the risk of some types of cancer, a disease associated with many factors.

Psyllium (pronounced "silly-um") is a seed, grown commercially in India. Its husk is used as a bulk forming laxative in numerous products, and Constance Kies, PhD, in a 1982 issue of Prevention wrote:

> "As it absorbs water in the digestive tract, the Psyllium
> expands, stimulating and speeding up elimination."

Psyllium also looks as though it is a cholesterol fighter, as Kies found in an experiment with healthy volunteers whose cholesterol levels dropped, on average, from 193 to 168 when they added Psyllium to their customary diets.

Gastroenterologist Jack D. Welsh, MD at the University of Oklahoma Health Sciences Centre, noted in the June, 1982 edition of the American Journal of Clinical Nutrition that Psyllium entirely prevented the expected gas pain and nausea.

If Psyllium seed powder is added to the husk powder in the proper ratio exactly how Life Force does, the preparation becomes an intestinal cleanser. The Psyllium seed fragments are very hard; they tend to scrape away the toxic plaque off the walls and clean it away over a period of months.

The purpose of the Intestinal Product is to provide the bulk necessary to create a natural cleansing of the intestines and colon, eliminating both waste matter and mucous build-up while allowing the intestines better to absorb nutrients. It also absorbs fats and cholesterol and promotes the peristaltic action of the colon. It is gentle and effective in helping the body return to its natural, healthy functions.

You may purchase an Herbal Colon Cleanse from:

www.therapies.com/acatalog

DIET

This book would also be incomplete if it did not make you aware of the main cause of colon disorders. I have therefore homed in on the three types of food that create problems in your digestive system:

Meat

When we look at our diet and what is good and bad for us, it is always beneficial to look at the way our ancestors used to eat. What has been eaten for 100,000s of years has determined the ability of our body to digest certain food. It will take another few thousand years (at best) before our body is able to digest the junk food some people ingest nowadays.

Prior to the Second World War, meat was expensive and most people only ate it on special occasions or at weekends (if they could afford it). Nowadays, some people eat meat several times a week. Sometimes, several times a day. Mr Richard McDonald[1] and Ray Kroc have probably affected the health of more people than were killed during the Second World War by introducing their fast food restaurants.

Should we really eat meat?

To answer this question, let's consider the following facts:

- Our teeth tell us that we *should* not eat much meat. Our molars and premolars are for grinding and crushing. Carnivores have teeth that are sharp and pointed, made to tear the flesh of other animals.
- Our saliva contains ptyalin and is alkaline for the digestion of starches. Carnivore's saliva is acid for the digestion of animal food.

---

[1] *You have probably heard of these fast food restaurants* ☺

45

- Our digestive system is 30 feet (10 metres) in length to allow the slow absorption of all the nutrients we eat. A carnivore's digestive system is short (only about 3 times the length of their trunk), meat does not get a chance to stagnate and stick to the walls.
- A carnivore's stomach generates ten times as much hydrochloric acid as ours does for the digestion of meat.
- The digestion of meat generates Uric acid. Our liver cannot easily eliminate Uric acid. A carnivore's liver can eliminate ten to fifteen times more Uric acid than ours can.

Where will I get my protein?

This is a standard question when I tell people to cut down or entirely give up meat.

Firstly, we must learn that we do not just absorb protein from meat. In order for our body to create protein from meat, it must first break the animal protein down into amino acids and then manufacture human protein with these. This procedure is very tiring on the body and extremely inefficient.

Where do you think horses, elephants, cows, sheep etc.. get their protein from? Yes, you've got it: from the grass, vegetation and all the plants they eat.

Secondly, let's clear the misconception about the importance of protein in our diet. The information originates from tests that were conducted on rats. Rats need up to eleven times as much protein as we need in our diet as is illustrated by analysing rat mother's milk. So relax, you are not going to die from a lack of protein if you cut down on your meat eating habit.

One of my main Macrobiotic teachers, Denny Waxman, used to tell us that the body manufactures protein from just about any food and that we could not be lacking protein unless we stopped eating or were malnourished. This is confirmed by research done in 1957[2] confirming that nearly all the complex carbohydrates, such as those in whole grains, beans or potatoes, have amino acid profiles adequate for human protein needs.

On the subject of protein, it is interesting to learn that in Macrobiotics, we are also told that cancers feed on protein and that we should always restrict the amount of protein in a cancer patient's diet.

Some will argue that fat is necessary because it is a source of linoleic acid. As this acid is also contained in brown rice, the body will get an ample supply by following the diet described in this book and this will not be a problem.

Where else can I get protein from?

If you are still worried about your protein intake, the following foods have a high content of easily absorbed amino acid suitable for the production of human protein:

Peas, lentils, chick peas, kidney beans, fish, tofu, green grapes, iceberg lettuce, collards and kale.

What is the effect of meat on the body?

These days meat is usually frozen, overcooked and as such stripped of all its goodness. It gives an immediate burst of energy and strength. This is OK in colder and Polar Regions if you do not mix the meat (Yang) with sweet (Yin) food, otherwise it is unhealthy in the long term.

An excess of meat will cause problems of accumulation of matter: clogged vessels and organs, putrefaction and infection. As soon as the animal is killed, meat starts to putrefy. This process is nowadays

---

[2] *Rose, W. "The amino acid requirements of adult man" - Nutritional abstracts and reviews*

controlled by the use of freezing that allows us to eat animals killed several days, weeks, months or years ago (as recent TV programs informed us).

Putrefaction resumes when the meat is unfrozen i.e. just before you start eating it. To properly digest meat takes 3 to 5 days and as much as two weeks in the elderly[3]. This is compared with a proper digestion time of one to one and half days for non-meat eaters.

Should you eat meat on a regular basis, your intestines are never clear and the meat putrefies in your digestive track. Putrefaction produces toxins and amines that accumulate in the liver, kidneys and large intestines, destroys bacterial cultures (especially those that synthesise vitamin B complex) and causes degeneration of the villi of the small intestine.

Saturated fatty acid accumulates in and around vital organs and blood vessels, often leading to cysts, tumours, and hardening of the arteries. Saturated fat also raises the amount of cholesterol in the blood. Over a period of several years, putrefied meat is going to adhere to the lining of your intestines and cause various problems such as IBS[4], stomach cramps, prolapsed colons, haemorrhoids, constipation, diverticulosis, appendicitis, varicose veins, atherosclerosis and colon cancer etc...

To compensate for eating meat, the body needs more oxygen in the bloodstream. The breathing rate rises after eating animal food making it difficult to maintain a calm mind. Thinking becomes defensive, suspicious, rigid and sometimes aggressive. A very analytical view is often the result.

---

[3] *Personal Macrobiotic notes and also in: Walker, A R P, Burkitt & Painter - Lancet medical journal, "Effects of Dietary fibre on stools and transit times, and its role in the causation of disease" -1972*

[4] *Irritable Bowel Syndrome. This condition seems to be freely diagnosed for whatever intestinal problems doctors are unsure of these days.*

It makes the muscles slack and the joints stiff. Daily consumption of meat and dairy food, is at the core of our excessive protein intake, which has been associated with dehydration and heat stroke in athletes, fatal exacerbation of kidney and liver malfunctions, increased acidity of body fluids, infant deaths, premature aging, heart disease, and cancer. A high protein intake creates toxic by-products in the form of unused nitrogen; excreting these can seriously overtax the kidneys, unless large amounts of water is drunk to flush them out.

The saturated fat content of meat will then start circulating in your blood stream and start coating your arteries and eventually various organs eventually leading to the development of serious disease such as cancer or heart problems.

In the United States these days, 2 out of every 3 people suffer from some form of serious problems related to that very high intake of fat.

"The average American & European intestine carries over 5 pounds of putrid, half digested red meat, plus another 5-10 pounds of foul toxic mucous waste impacted over years in the folds of the colon and small intestines."[5]

When the actor John Wayne died, an autopsy revealed that his intestines had grown to 12" (30 cms) in diameter with only a small opening in the middle to allow the digestive process to painfully carry on.

What else is in the meat I eat?

This is one of the problems. Nowadays, the meat that you buy contains a lot of chemicals that you end up eating when you consume your favourite dish:

Antibiotics and steroids in the feed to prevent infections and increase weight quickly. This has had the effect of causing the development of

---

[5] *www.hps-online.com/bcc1htm (The Colon Cleansing Story)*

new disease breeding bacteria, resistant to many forms of antibiotics and causing a threat to human life.

Also, sex hormones such as androgens, progestogens and estrogens to promote faster growth. The long term effects associated with the consumption of these are:

Obesity, infertility, diabetes, dwarfism, gigantism, kidney disease, hypertension, precocious puberty, hypoglycaemia, masculinisation of females, feminisation of males and cancer.

Dairy food

It always amazes me to find out that, despite numerous articles to the contrary, a large percentage of my students still believe that dairy food is healthy and necessary for strong bones. I should not be surprised though, the dairy food industry is spending enough money to make us believe we are doing our body a lot of good by eating/drinking their products.

It is interesting to notice that human beings are the only animals on this planet that keep on drinking milk after they have been weaned off their mother's breast milk. In the words of Dr Michael Klaper MD:

> "It's not natural for humans to drink cow's milk. Human milk is for humans. Cow's milk is for calves. You have no more need of cow's milk than you do rat's milk, horse's milk or elephant's milk. Cow's milk is a high fat fluid exquisitely designed to turn a 65 lb baby calf into a 400 lb cow. That's what cow's milk is for!"

How do you think cows, sheep, horses etc.. keep their bones strong? Yes, by eating their greens (grass).

Mother's milk versus cow's milk?

Why is it that we believe that because something is good for a new-born calf, it is good for us? Don't we realise that the genetics of a calf are different from ours?

- It takes 45 days for a calf to double its weight
- It takes 180 days for a human to double its weight
- Cow's milk has three times more protein than mother's milk
- Cow's milk has almost four times more calcium than mother's milk[6]
- A cow will grow to three to four times the size of an adult and the above differences are ideal for that animal to grow
- Cow's milk only has 50% of the carbohydrate of human milk.
- Cow's milk contains 3 times as much sodium as human milk.
- The protein in cow's milk is mainly casein. This is poorly assimilated in the human body.

According to Dr. John R. Christopher, N.D., M.H., there is up to 20 times more casein in cow's milk than human milk which makes the nutrients in cow's milk difficult (if not impossible) for humans to assimilate.

Another factor is that to absorb calcium properly, the body needs a similar quantity of **magnesium**. As dairy does not contain a sufficient quantity of magnesium, only 25% of the calcium is absorbed. The body uses calcium to build the mortar on arterial walls, which becomes atherosclerotic plaques. The surplus calcium is then converted into kidney stones. Excess of calcium also leads to arthritis and gout.

Magnesium is critical to proper neural and muscular function and to maintaining proper pH balance in the body. Magnesium, along with

---

[6] *Food and Healing by Annmarie Colbin*

vitamin B6 (pyridoxine), helps to dissolve calcium phosphate stones that often accumulate from excesses of dairy intake.

Yet another factor is the **phosphorus** calcium ratio:

"only foods with a calcium to phosphorus ratio of two to one or better should be used as a primary source of calcium[7]". The reason for this is that the phosphorus can mix with calcium in the digestive track and prevent the absorption of calcium.

The fat content in cow's milk is only about 10% higher than in mother's milk. Isn't it amazing that this is the only thing we have changed in cow's milk?

Does milk prevent bone fractures?

Let's get this most commonly asked question out of the way first.

Many people believe that if they stop eating calf's food, their bones will collapse in a heap. There could be nothing further from the truth.

In a 12 years Harvard study of 78,000 nurses who drank three or more glasses of milk per day did not reduce fractures at all[8]. An Australian study showed the same thing[9].

The fact is that the more dairy people consumed, the more likely they are to suffer hip fractures. People in North America and Northern Europe break two or three times more bones than people in Asian and

---

[7] *Dr Frank Oski - chairman of the department of Paediatric at Upstate Medical Centre, State University of New York in Syracuse. Author of "Don't drink you milk"*

[8] *The Harvard Nurse's study - Cumming & Klineberg, published in the American Journal of Epidemiology*

[9] *Australian study - Feskanich, published in the American Journal of Public Health*

African countries who have the lowest calcium intake[10]. Europe and North America consume the highest levels of dairy foods in the world.

In the USA, one in two women and one in eight men over age 50 breaks a bone because of osteoporosis[11]. In China where people eat less than half the calcium recommended by the USDA and seem healthy, among women over 50, the hip fracture rate appeared to be one fifth as high as in Western nations.

The problem is not so much that we do not get enough calcium. It is that we lose too much calcium. This happens when we eat regular portions of meat, poultry, eggs or dairy products[12]. All these products increase acidity in the body and.. *the body's way of getting rid of this acid is to draw on its reserve of calcium and other minerals from bones and teeth to make the blood more alkaline.*

Vegetarians will need about 50% less calcium than meat eaters because they lose much less calcium in their urine.

Here is the technical explanation from Dr Joseph Mercola web site at www.mercola.com:

> "Your bones are a mineral bank for your body storing 99 percent calcium, 85 percent phosphorus and 60 percent magnesium. When mineral levels are low in the blood, osteoclasts break down bone to free up these minerals and deposit them in the blood. Excessive animal protein intake increases the need for calcium to neutralise the acid formed from digesting animal protein. This indicates that the drinking of processed milk destroys bone in the process of digestion".

---

[10] *Dr. T. Colin Campbell, PhD, nutritional biochemist at Cornell University - on Osteoporosis*

[11] *Statistics from the "National Osteoporosis Foundation" USA*

[12] *"Does Milk really look good on you? Don't drink it!" from Idaho Observer at http://prolibertycom/observer/20000208.htm*

The following lists show the food that will in some way affect the calcium absorption in the body[13].

1. Dairy

    This is fully explained in this chapter.

2. Sugar

    The acid reaction is fully explained on the chapter on sugar that follows

3. High protein food

    The acid reaction is fully explained in the previous section on animal food and this section on dairy.

4. Wine, vinegar and citrus

    These are acid foods that also require the buffering action of calcium and other minerals to render the blood more alkaline.

6. Coffee, alcohol and salt

    "The loss of calcium is substantial for people who drink eight or more cups of coffee per day. Social drinkers run 2.5 the risk of developing osteoporosis as alcohol interferes with the absorption of calcium. As for salt: one study of Dutch students excreted 20% more calcium when they consumed 6,000 milligrams of sodium than when they only ingested 3,000 milligrams daily[14]".

    "Calcium in bones tends to dissolve into the bloodstream, then pass through the kidneys into the urine. Sodium (salt) in the foods you eat can greatly increase calcium loss through the kidneys.[15]"

---

[13] *Extracted from my notes on various Macrobiotic courses at the East West Centre London*

[14] *Food and Healing by Annemarie Colbin*

[15] *Nordin BEC, Need AG, Morris HA, Horowitz M. The nature and significance of the relationship between urinary sodium and urinary calcium in women. J Nutr 1993;123:1615-22.*

If you reduce your sodium intake to one to two grams per day, you will hold onto calcium better. To do that, avoid salty snack foods and canned goods with added sodium, and keep salt use low on the stove and at the table.

The best way to prevent osteoporosis

Osteoporosis is often described as brittle bones through lack of calcium. Calcium will first be lost from the spine and the pelvic area and up to 40% calcium may have been lost before osteoporosis is diagnosed[16]

What is Calcium?

Calcium is about 1.5 to 2% of the weight of an adult body.

About 99% of the calcium is concentrated in the bones and the teeth. The remaining 1% can be found in the soft tissues and body fluids.

Calcium is used for the clotting of blood, the action of some enzymes and the interchange of body fluid through the cell walls.

Calcium helps the heart beat smoothly.

If calcium is low, the nerves become irritable.

Mixed with phosphorous, calcium gives rigidity to our skeleton and teeth.

Phosphorus and vitamin D are necessary for the proper absorption of calcium.

---

[16] *Herman Aihara - "Acid and Alkaline"*

What food contains calcium?

The following table lists some of the food with high calcium content. It is in descending sequence, showing the food with the highest source of calcium first:

VEGETABLES	SEEDS	SEAWEEDS[17]
Parsley	Sesame seeds (second highest content of all)	Hiziki (highest content of all)
Collards	Almonds	Wakame
Dandelion greens	Brazil nuts	Kombu
Kale	Walnuts roasted	Agar agar
Turnip greens	Peanuts roasted	Dulse
Watercress	Raisins	
Broccoli		
Okra		

According to Dr. Neal Barnard, author of *Turn Off the Fat Genes* (2001) and several other books on diet and health, calcium absorption from vegetables such as broccoli, Brussels sprouts, mustard greens, turnip greens, kale, and some other leafy green vegetables range between 40 percent and 64 percent. Calcium absorption from dairy is a poor 30% and with the many problems we now know.

On www.milsucks.com researchers report on the best way to get strong bones:

---

[17] *These can be used in cooking and mixed with vegetables and beans. They provide an excellent source of minerals in the diet.*

- Getting enough vitamin D (if you don't spend at least 15 minutes in the sun every day, be sure to take <u>good Vitamin and Mineral supplements</u>.

- Eliminating animal protein (for a variety of reasons, animal protein causes severe bone deterioration).

- Limiting alcohol consumption (alcohol is toxic to the cells that form bones and inhibits the absorption of calcium).

- Limiting salt intake (sodium leaches calcium out of the bones)

- Not smoking (studies have shown that women who smoke one pack of cigarettes a day have 5 to 10 percent less bone density at menopause than non-smokers).

    A study of identical twins showed that, if one twin had been a long-term smoker and the other had not, the smoker had more than a 40 percent higher risk of a fracture[18].

- Getting plenty of exercise. Studies have concluded that physical exercise is the key to building strong bones (more important than any other factor). For example, a study published in the *British Medical Journal*, which followed 1,400 men and women over a 15-year period, found that exercise may be the best protection against hip fractures and that "reduced intake of dietary calcium does not seem to be a risk factor." And Penn State University researchers found that bone density is significantly affected by how much exercise girls get during their teen years, when 40 to 50 percent of their skeletal mass is developed. Consistent with previous research, the Penn State study, which was published in *Pediatrics* (2000), the journal of the American Academy of Pediatrics, showed that calcium intake, which ranged from 500 to 1,500 mg per day, has no lasting effect on bone health. "We (had)

---

[18] *Hopper JL, Seeman E. The bone density of female twins discordant for tobacco use. N Engl J Med 1994;330:387-92.*

hypothesized that increased calcium intake would result in better adolescent bone gain. Needless to say, we were surprised to find our hypothesis refuted," one researcher explained."

What about dairy food and cancer?

A study published in 1989 showed that in Scandinavia and the Netherlands (two areas with higher milk consumption) also had higher breast cancer rates.

World-wide, men seem far more likely to die of prostate cancer in countries where dairy consumption is high than in countries where it is low. A study published in 1977 revealed that 10 men die of prostate cancer in Western Europe for every one who dies in Asia.

Several cancers, such as ovarian cancer, have been linked to the consumption of dairy products. The milk sugar lactose is broken down in the body into another sugar, galactose. In turn, galactose is broken down further by enzymes. According to a study by Daniel Cramer, M.D., and his colleagues at Harvard[19], when dairy product consumption exceeds the enzymes' capacity to break down galactose, it can build up in the blood and may affect a woman's ovaries. Some women have particularly low levels of these enzymes, and when they consume dairy products on a regular basis, their risk of ovarian cancer can be triple that of other women.[20]

Recommended Ebook: <u>Richardson Cancer Diet – Alternative Cancer treatment</u>

---

[19] *Cramer DW, Harlow BL, Willet WC. Galactose consumption and metabolism in relation to the risk of ovarian cancer. Lancet 1989;2:66-71.*

[20] *www.pcrm.org on Dairy*

What else is bad in the dairy food I eat?

Milk contains no fibre or complex carbohydrates and is laden with saturated fat and cholesterol.

As read in the www.notmilk.com newsletter on 27 February 2002:

"ALL cow's milk has 59 active hormones, scores of allergens, fat and cholesterol. Most cow's milk has measurable quantities of herbicides, pesticides, dioxin's (up to 2,200 times the safe levels), up to 52 powerful antibiotics, blood, pus, faeces, bacteria and viruses. (Cow's milk can have traces of anything the cow ate... including such things as radioactive fallout from nuke testing ... (the 50's strontium-90 problem)."

ONE cubic centimetre (cc) of commercial cow's milk is allowed to have up to 750,000 somatic cells (common name is "PUS") and 20,000 live bacteria... before it is kept off the market. That amounts to a whopping 20 million live squiggly bacteria and up to 750 MILLION pus cells per litre[21].

Some of the most staggering information I read came from a newsletter from www.notmilk.com on 28 February 2002:

"The current issue of Hoard's Dairyman, (Volume 147, number 4), the self proclaimed "National Dairy Farm Magazine," contains information that surprised even me.

Ads are supposed to promote products, and I suppose this one does. It advertises a test for one very serious cow disease. This ad most certainly does not promote the dairy industry's objective of trying to convince you that their product is wholesome.

The editors of the February 25, 2002 issue must have been counting ad revenue and ignoring possible repercussions from the half-page advertisement that appears on page 150. The ad shows cows in a field, and challenges the reader in a bold type statement:

---

[21] *www.notmilk.com newsletter on 27 February 2002*

"You Can't Tell By Looking"

The text of the ad reveals that "most dairy herds are affected by bovine leukaemia virus."

What? America drinks body fluids from cows with leukaemia?

I knew that bovine leukaemia is a problem, but I had no idea of the extent of that problem.

According to the ad, 89% of the dairy herds in the United States have cows infected with leukaemia."

Would you believe it? 89% of the cows in America are infected with leukaemia! Does this means that 9 times out of 10 when you eat the meat or drink the milk from a cow, you are eating cancer cells? Not quite, pasteurisation (if done properly) should remove the infection. But, the question is: is the pasteurisation process done properly?

Growth hormone for cows[22] in the USA?

Fifty years ago, the average cow produced 20,000 pounds of milk every year. Today, top producing bovines are producing 50,000 pounds per year. This dramatic increase is due to antibiotics, drugs and recombinant Bovine Growth Hormone (rBGH)[23]. The use of rBGH can cause udder infections in our bovine. So, more antibiotics are given to the poor animals. This and the pesticides ingested by the animal find their way to our plates and glasses[24].

---

[22] *Apart from this growth hormone, the average cow is commonly fed a mixture of steroids, antibiotics, human sewage, sawdust, concrete dust and paper to fatten them up*

[23] *Produced by the Monsanto Corporation (the massive company who wants to feeds us genetic food and mass produced the poisonous DDT)*

[24] *British medical journal the "Lancet" - Cows milk as a cause of infantile colic with breast-fed infants. - 1978*

"The milk from cows treated with rBGH contains elevated levels insulin-like growth factor-1 (IGF-1), one of the most powerful growth factors ever identified. While IGF-1 doesn't cause cancer, it definitely stimulates its growth. Recent studies have found a seven-fold increase in the risk of breast cancer in women with the highest IGF-1 levels, and a four-fold increase in prostate cancer in men with the highest levels of IGF-1.

In 1995 researchers at the National Institutes of Health reported that IGF-1 plays a central role in the progression of many childhood cancers and in the growth of tumours in breast cancer, small cell lung cancer, melanoma, and cancers of the pancreas and prostate. In September 1997 an international team of researchers reported the first epidemiological evidence that high IGF-1 concentrations are closely linked to an increased risk of prostate cancer. The effects of IGF-1 concentrations on prostate cancer risk were found to be astoundingly large - much higher than for any other known risk factor. Men having an IGF-1 level between approximately 300 and 500 ng/mL were found to have more than four times the risk of developing prostate cancer than did men with a level between 100 and 185 ng/mL[25]."

The good news is that the European Union has a ban on IGF-1 treated cows. Keep an eye on the news if you live in the UK though. We are never far behind the USA...

What is the effect of milk on the body?

Dairy food contributes a soothing, stabilising and overall calming influence on the digestive and nervous system. However it can lead to illness in its own right or in combination with other factors.

Casein, the protein in cheese, milk, cream, butter and other dairy foods cannot be assimilated easily and begins to accumulate in an undigested state in the upper intestine, putrefying, producing toxins,

---

[25] *www.mercola.com by Dr Joseph Mercola*

and leading to a weakening of the gastric, intestinal, pancreatic and biliary systems as well as mucous deposits[26].

The inability to digest milk or other dairy products is known as lactose intolerance[27] and is found in about 25 to 90% of the world's population.

Dairy food affects the breast, uterus, ovaries, prostate, thyroid, nasal cavities, pituitary gland, the cochlea in the ear, and the cerebral area surrounding the mid brain. Its adverse affects first appear as an accumulation of mucus and fat and then the formation of cysts, tumours and finally cancer. Many people who eat or have eaten dairy food have an accumulation of mucus in the nasal cavities and inner ear often resulting in hay fever and hearing problems.

Consumption of dairy food leads to stones in the kidney and the gallbladder, the development of breast cysts and tumours and finally breast cancer. In Asia, where many people drink no milk at all, breast cancer tends to be rare. In rural China, for example, among women aged 35 to 64, Campbell found that breast cancer deaths averaged 8.7 per 100,000, as opposed to 44 per 100,000 in the US, about a 5-fold difference.

Other problems include vaginal discharges, ovarian cysts, fibrosis and uterine cancer, ovarian cancer and prostate fat accumulation including infertility. Mucous accumulation in the lungs can cause breathing difficulties and possible asthma. This with tobacco traps tars which may lead to cancer of the lungs. Other problems include cramps, diarrhoea, allergies, iron deficiency, and aggressive and antisocial

---

[26] *I always tell Mums who come to see me reporting their child has an ear infection, runny nose, sinus infections, chronic coughs or asthma to stop dairy products. The results are amazing.*

[27] *The body enzyme "lactase" is necessary to digest lactose. Most people (except those of Northern European origin, vegetarian Hindus and Berbers) stop producing this enzyme when they are weaned off and become lactose intolerant.*

behaviour. Atherosclerosis, heart attacks, arthritis, several forms of cancer and type 1 diabetes[28].

According to a report published by the American Academy of Allergy and Immunology Committee on Adverse Reactions to Food (part of the National Institutes of Health), the allergies of up to one third of children tested cleared after milk was removed from their diet.

Are other dairy products safer than milk?

Each bite of hard cheese has TEN TIMES whatever was in that sip of milk... because it takes ten pounds of milk to make one pound of cheese. Each bite of ice cream has 12 times ... and every swipe of butter 21 times whatever is contained in the fat molecules in a sip of milk.

What do scientists say about dairy?

Dr. T. Colin Campbell, PhD, a prestigious nutritional biochemist at Cornell University states:

- The ultimate problem with cow's milk is that nature concocts different formulas of mother's milk for different species. What's good for baby calves isn't necessarily good for human babies or adults. "Isn't it strange that we're the only species that suckles from another species?"

- Dr. Campbell theorises that cow's milk unnaturally stimulates enzymes and growth hormones in the human body that increase the risk of various diseases.

---

[28] *Several Epidemiological studies have shown a strong correlation between the use of dairy products and the occurrence of insulin-dependent diabetes. Research in 1992 (by Karjalainen J, Martin JM, Knip M - "A bovine albumin peptide as a possible trigger of insulin-dependent diabetes mellitus" - N Engl J Med 1992;327:302-7.) found that a specific dairy protein sparks an auto-immune reaction, which is believed to be what destroys the insulin-producing cells of the pancreas.*

- He has also come to the conclusion that cow's milk may not even do what it is supposed to do best - build strong bones, since recent studies suggest that humans may need less calcium for strong bones than was once believed. Additionally, other foods, including various vegetables and legumes, may be a better source than cow's milk.

In 1965, Dr. Campbell worked as co-ordinator of a US Aid project in the Philippines, where poverty stricken children were dying mysteriously from liver cancer believed to be linked to malnutrition. However, to his surprise, Campbell discovered that the incidence of liver cancer was especially high among some of the best nourished kids, whose diets were supplemented with powdered milk provided through a US subsidised program. He was completely baffled until he read about a 1968 research study conducted in India and published in the Archives of Pathology (Arch Pathol 1968 Feb;85(2):133-7), which linked a milk protein to liver cancer in lab rats[29].

Homogenisation and Pasteurisation

Milk is typically pasteurised more than once to kill off the germs before it gets to your table... each time for only 15 seconds at 162 degrees Fahrenheit.

This process unfortunately also kills the enzymes that would allow us to better digest the stuff and also gets rid of some 50% of the vitamins. Several studies have demonstrated that calves that were fed their mother's milk that had been pasteurised died within 60 days. Don't you just love it!

---

[29] *www.mercola.com*

Raw, unpasteurised, milk contains beneficial bacteria such as lactobacillus acidolphilus, which holds putrefactive bacteria in check.

You may ask yourself by now: Why do we bother to pasteurise?

The answer to this is very simple:

1. It allows farmers and suppliers to keep the milk longer before it goes bad.
2. It allows farmers to have slacker standards of cleanliness

Homogenisation breaks up large milk molecules into small ones allowing them to get into the bloodstream! This becomes an expressway for any fat-borne toxins (lead, dioxin's, etc.) into your (otherwise) most protected organs. Without homogenisation, large fat molecules cannot get through the intestinal wall into the bloodstream.

Kurt Oster, M.D. of Bridgeport, Connecticut declared that homogenisation, by breaking up the molecules into smaller pieces, allows some substances to pass through the intestinal wall unchanged by the digestive process. One of these substances is an enzyme called xanthine oxydase, or XO, normally found in the milk fat, which helps in the breakdown of protein. After passing through the intestinal wall and being picked up by the lymphatic system it ends up in the bloodstream. As it courses through the arteries, it scratches and corrodes the inside of the walls, causing small primary lesions. As a defence against this, the body deposits fibrin and cholesterol (lipoprotein) over the lesions to avoid further damage.

This process together with the common fortifying of milk with vitamin D further encourages the deposit of calcium in the arteries. This is one of the reason why people are suffering from hardening of the arteries at a young age.

Statistics

"In 1981 Stephen Seely... obtained mortality data from the World Health Organisation... and calculated correlation coefficients for various foods and food components... comparing quantity consumed with mortality rates from different countries... (Seely) found that milk and milk products gave the highest correlation coefficient, while sugar, animal proteins and animal fats came in second, third, and fourth, respectively.[30]"

Sugar

There are 4 types of sugars:

1. Complex sugars or polysaccharides (found in beans, vegetables and grains)

2. Double sugars or disaccharides (found in cane sugar (sucrose) and milk (lactose))

3. Simple sugars or monosaccharides (found in fruits (fructose) and honey)

4. Artificial sugar (known as sweeteners)

1. Polysaccharides

Polysaccharides are first decomposed by saliva in the mouth, then further down in the stomach and then completely digested in the duodenum and intestines. Brown rice, grains, beans, vegetables are polysaccharides.

2. Disaccharides

Most manufactured or processed food today contains sucrose or an artificial form of sugar. Refined sugar is completely void of any useful nutrient. Sucrose is labelled as a "carbohydrate". This is highly convenient when manufacturers of certain foods wish to hide the sugar

---

[30] *Seely, Diet and Coronary Disease, A Survey of Mortality Rates and Food Consumption Statistics of 24 Countries, Medical Hypothesis 7:907-918, 1981*

content of some of their products. They simply label it as containing "carbohydrates".

When refined sugar enters the stomach, it causes what is known as a sugar reaction where the stomach is paralysed. As little as a quarter teaspoon can cause this. Since refined sugar is strongly alkaloid, the stomach will secrete an unusually high amount of acid to make balance. If this process is repeated over a long period of time, an ulceration of the walls of the stomach will occur.

Our blood normally maintains a weak alkaline condition, and when strongly alkaline sugar is introduced, the acid reaction takes place causing the bloodstream to become over acidic. To compensate for this our internal supply of minerals is mobilised so as to restore a normal balance. The minerals in our daily food and reserves should be sufficient to cope with the situation. However is we eat refined sugar daily, this supply soon runs out and we must depend on minerals stored deep within the body, particularly calcium, magnesium, sodium and potassium in our bones and teeth. If this continues for a long enough period, the depletion of calcium from the bones and teeth results in their eventual decay and general weakening and osteoporosis.

The body has various back up systems when minerals are in short supply and the blood is acidic. One of them is called the "Ammonia buffer". The kidneys start producing Ammonia which is a strong alkali (ph 9.25). This balances the ph once again. Unfortunately, if the intake of sugar carries on, there will result a depletion of minerals from the bones and the teeth and the "Ammonia buffer" will eventually damage the kidneys with too much ammonia and acid.

Excess sugar is stored in various places within the body, first in the form of glycogen in the liver. When the amount of glycogen exceeds the liver's storage capacity of about 50g, it is then released into the bloodstream in the form of fatty acid, which is stored in the more inactive places of the body such as the buttocks, thighs and mid section. Then if the intake of refined sugar is continued, this fatty acid becomes attracted to the more active organs such as the heart and the kidneys, which gradually become encased in a layer of fat and mucus, which also penetrate the inner tissues of these organs. This of course weakens their normal function and when excessive enough causes their eventual stoppage.

This excessive intake of sugar in modern society can be seen in the increasing incidence of such degenerative diseases as heart disease, which two out of five people in the US are now suffering from. Refined sugar also directly affects our thinking abilities through the destruction of the intestinal bacteria which are responsible for the creation of B-Vitamins necessary for the synthesis of glutamic acid which is directly involved in the mental activities carried on the brain. A lack of this component can result in a lack of memory and ability to think clearly.

Constant sugar consumption has also been linked to Parkinson and Alzheimer's disease. Complete removal from the diet has seen stunning recoveries from cancer. diabetes and heart illnesses[31].

Dr Joseph Mercola[32] wrote these comments on sugar:

"Another reason to avoid sugar is to slow down the aging process. If you want to stay young it is very important to limit sugar to the smallest amount possible. It is the most significant physical factor that accelerates aging. It is a negative fountain of youth. It does this by two mechanisms. The first is to actually attach itself to proteins in the body forming a new sugar-protein substance called advanced glycation end-products (AGEs). The higher the AGE levels, the faster you are aging. As this study points out, sugar also increases free radicals in the body which also accelerate the ageing process."

---

[31] *Sweet and Dangerous by Yudkin J - Bantham book*

[32] *www.mercola.com - highly recommended web site with free newsletter*

The 1931 Nobel laureate in medicine, German Otto Warburg, Ph.D., discovered that glucose is used as a fuel by cancer. Do you really want to feed your cancer cells?

A personal story:

I used to teach at adult education centres in the UK. I love waffles sweetened with maize syrup. One night, I made a mistake and bought a packet sweetened with honey (a very strong form of sugar). I could not put two sentences together during my course. My words would not come out and I felt completely spaced out. This is the effect of sugar if you are not used to it.

On his wonderful web site, Dr Joseph Mercola[33] headed one of his pages "78 Ways Sugar Can Ruin Your Health". With kind permission (http://www.mercola.com/), it is reproduced below:

1. Sugar can suppress the immune system.
2. Sugar can upset the body's mineral balance.
3. Sugar can cause hyperactivity, anxiety, concentration difficulties, and crankiness in children.
4. Sugar can cause drowsiness and decreased activity in children.
5. Sugar can adversely affect children's school grades.
6. Sugar can produce a significant rise in triglycerides.
7. Sugar contributes to a weakened defence against bacterial infection.
8. Sugar can cause kidney damage.
9. Sugar can reduce helpful high-density cholesterol (HDLs).
10. Sugar can promote an elevation of harmful cholesterol (LDLs).
11. Sugar may lead to chromium deficiency.
12. Sugar can cause copper deficiency.
13. Sugar interferes with absorption of calcium and magnesium.

---

[33] *www.mercola.com - highly recommended web site with free newsletter*

14. Sugar may lead to cancer of the breast, ovaries, prostate, and rectum.
15. Sugar can cause colon cancer, with an increased risk in women.
16. Sugar can be a risk factor in gall bladder cancer.
17. Sugar can increase fasting levels of blood glucose.
18. Sugar can weaken eyesight.
19. Sugar raises the level of a neurotransmitter called serotonin, which can narrow blood vessels.
20. Sugar can cause hypoglycaemia.
21. Sugar can produce an acidic stomach.
22. Sugar can raise adrenaline levels in children.
23. Sugar can increase the risk of coronary heart disease.
24. Sugar can speed the ageing process, causing wrinkles and grey hair.
25. Sugar can lead to alcoholism.
26. Sugar can promote tooth decay.
27. Sugar can contribute to weight gain and obesity.
28. High intake of sugar increases the risk of Crohn's disease and ulcerative colitis.
29. Sugar can cause a raw, inflamed intestinal tract in persons with gastric or duodenal ulcers.
30. Sugar can cause arthritis
31. Sugar can cause asthma.
32. Sugar can cause candidiasis (yeast infection).
33. Sugar can lead to the formation of gallstones.
34. Sugar can lead to the formation of kidney stones.
35. Sugar can cause ischemic heart disease.
36. Sugar can cause appendicitis.
37. Sugar can exacerbate the symptoms of multiple sclerosis.
38. Sugar can indirectly cause haemorrhoids.
39. Sugar can cause varicose veins.
40. Sugar can elevate glucose and insulin responses in oral contraception users.

41. Sugar can lead to periodontal disease.
42. Sugar can contribute to osteoporosis.
43. Sugar contributes to saliva acidity.
44. Sugar can cause a decrease in insulin sensitivity.
45. Sugar leads to decreased glucose tolerance.
46. Sugar can decrease growth hormone.
47. Sugar can increase total cholesterol.
48. Sugar can increase systolic blood pressure.
49. Sugar can change the structure of protein causing interference with protein absorption.
50. Sugar causes food allergies.
51. Sugar can contribute to diabetes.
52. Sugar can cause toxaemia during pregnancy.
53. Sugar can contribute to eczema in children.
54. Sugar can cause cardiovascular disease.
55. Sugar can impair the structure of DNA.
56. Sugar can cause cataracts.
57. Sugar can cause emphysema.
58. Sugar can cause atherosclerosis.
59. Sugar can cause free radical formation in the bloodstream.
60. Sugar lowers the enzymes' ability to function.
61. Sugar can cause loss of tissue elasticity and function.
62. Sugar can cause liver cells to divide, increasing the size of the liver.
63. Sugar can increase the amount of fat in the liver.
64. Sugar can increase kidney size and produce pathological changes in the kidney.
65. Sugar can overstress the pancreas, causing damage.
66. Sugar can increase the body's fluid retention.
67. Sugar can cause constipation.
68. Sugar can cause myopia (nearsightedness).
69. Sugar can compromise the lining of the capillaries.
70. Sugar can cause hypertension.
71. Sugar can cause headaches, including migraines.

72. Sugar can cause an increase in delta, alpha and theta brain waves, which can alter the mind's ability to think clearly.
73. Sugar can cause depression.
74. Sugar can increase insulin responses in those consuming high-sugar diets compared to low sugar diets.
75. Sugar increases bacterial fermentation in the colon.
76. Sugar can cause hormonal imbalance.
77. Sugar can increase blood platelet adhesiveness, which increases risk of blood clots.
78. Sugar increases the risk of Alzheimer Disease.

Do you really want to damage your body this much? or are you strong willed enough to give up sugar?

3. Monosaccharides

This is easily converted in our body into glucose (blood sugar). As fruits are concerned, it is however advisable to stick to local fruits. These belong to our environment and are easily digestible. Local fruits to the UK are pears, apples, strawberries, any form of berries, cherries etc..

Tropical fruits such as bananas, oranges, pineapple, papaya, mangoes etc.. do not belong to the UK climate and should only be eaten in great moderation as they are more difficult to excrete and will cause an accumulation of mucous in the upper respiratory track and affect the nervous system.

A story written by one of my patients[34] that demonstrates the negative effects of too much tropical fruit:

---

[34] *Ms Sally C*

"I had an illness relating to neurology which affected my vocal chords[35]. I went to see my doctor who prescribed antibiotics that were not successful. The so-called virus returned and yet my doctor wanted me to take more antibiotics, I expressed my dissatisfaction and wanted to know why I was subject to these repetitive viruses.

Finally I went to see a private consultant who diagnosed my condition as <u>DYSTONIA</u> (trouble of the sympathetic and parasympathetic nerves). There are various forms of dystonia but the form I suffered from is very rare. In October 1996 I was admitted to the Radcliffe Hospital in Oxford. Test after test they could not determine what was causing my condition. I was given drugs that acted against my well being morally and I was depressive and very distressed.

Providence came my way. I was sent a prospectus by Know How (Education guidance) about courses in anatomy and physiology. I spotted Patrick Hamouy's name and phoned him originally about his courses. I somehow ended asking him if he could help me.

I saw Patrick Hamouy in September 1997 and I will never forget that day it seemed that I was born again. For the first time I was in front of someone who listened to me. It was a new form of diagnosis. He asked me about my background, historical data, lifestyle, all areas of my life until now. He analysed my present medication and its side effects. I was so impressed and so happy at last there was hope for me.

His methods are impressive because he presents the treatment (he will probably say that it is not a treatment, but a guideline for better health) very clearly by going through it with the client verbally and at the same time presenting written support for continued reference. The treatment is not necessarily quick in acting but for long term health. By following the macrobiotic way as advised by Patrick Hamouy I have experienced an improvement in my health.

---

[35] *Author's note: Sally was losing her voice. On a frequent basis, she could not talk as no sound would come out of her throat*

The role of diet in a macrobiotic way of life is crucial to the maintenance of one's health. For a period of three months I followed the diet religiously, phoning Patrick whenever I needed clarification about what to eat.

...

This diet has made me feel great in many ways. Not only do I feel good mentally and physically, but friends have commented that I look a lot perkier. My energy levels are up, I'm a happier person, more assertive and rarely suffer from colds and flu. Going up and down the stairs is no problem. I get up in the morning without the usual aches and pains and I feel like I have had a new lease of life. My original dystonia symptoms have now completely disappeared."

Author's note on the above:

Sally had read somewhere that 5 pieces of fruit a day was good for her health. This was basically the cause of her problem. I diagnosed her as having an excess of Yin. I suppressed most Yin food in her diet and recovery was very quick. Nobody ever said that eating 5 pieces of tropical fruit a day is good for health. What was said is that 5 pieces of vegetables and fruits a day is healthy. I would therefore advise on 1 or 2 pieces of local fruits and 3 or 4 portions of vegetables if you are healthy. If not, then seek advice from a macrobiotic consultant for your diet[36].

4. Artificial sugar (known as sweeteners)

Although sweeteners are used by most to lose weight, it is most interesting that The American Cancer Society (1986) documented the fact that persons using artificial sweeteners gain more weight than those who avoid them. An amazing fact!

---

[36] *See contacts at the end of this book*

Aspartame

Aspartame is sold under the names of NutraSweet, Equal, Spoonful, and Equal-Measure.

It was discovered accidentally in 1965 by James Schlatter (a chemist) working for G D Serle Company. Schlatter was originally testing an anti-ulcer drug.

It was opposed by neuroscientist Dr John Olney and Consumer attorney James Turner in August 1974 over its safety and the fraudulent way the research was originally carried out[37]. Olney reported that aspartame affects the neurological process in humans. He claimed that it "excites or stimulates the neural cells to death"[38]

It was eventually approved in 1981 for dry goods and in 1983 for carbonated drinks. This approval was once again strongly opposed by two FDA research scientists[39] who highlighted the fraudulent testing of Aspartame by G D Serle Company.

Despite pleas from other research scientists such as Dr Woodrow Monte, Director of the Food Science and Nutritional Laboratory at Arizona State University, Arthur Hull Hayes Jr. of the FDA approved the use of aspartame in carbonated water in 1983. Arthur Hull Hayes Jr then left the FDA to start a new rewarding position with ... G D Serle public Relation Company.

Aspartame accounts for over 75 percent of the adverse reactions to food additives reported to the US Food and Drug Administration (FDA).

---

[37] *One of the techniques used to falsify the studies was to cut tumours out of test animals and put them back in the study. Another technique used was to list animals that had actually died as surviving the study.*

[3838] *The Guardian newspaper on 20 July 1990*

[39] *Jacqueline Verrett and Adrian Gross*

The diseases linked to the use of aspartame are:

Memory loss, hormonal problems, epilepsy, Parkinson's disease, Alzheimer's disease, AIDS dementia, MS (Multiple sclerosis)[40]

And ...

headaches, nausea, vertigo, insomnia, numbness, blurred vision, blindness and other eye problems, memory loss, slurred speech, depression, personality changes, hyperactivity, stomach disorders, seizures, skin lesions, rashes, anxiety attacks, muscle cramping and joint pain, loss of energy, symptoms mimicking heart attacks, hearing loss and ear ringing, and loss or change of taste[41].

In 1981, Satya Dubey, an FDA statistician, stated that the brain tumour data on aspartame was so "worrisome" that he could not recommend approval of NutraSweet. In a two-year study conducted by the manufacturer of aspartame, twelve of the 320 rats fed a normal diet and aspartame developed brain tumours while none of the other rats had tumours.

It is interesting to note that the incidence of brain tumours in persons over 65 years of age has increased 67% between the years 1973 and 1990. Brain tumours in all age groups has jumped 10%.

Aspartame Consumer Safety Network, in an article from General Aviation News reported that Michael Collins, former pilot, suffered from seizures whenever he drank diet soda. When he stopped using aspartame products, he remained seizure-free. Over 600 pilots have reported symptoms including some who have reported suffering grand mal seizures in the cockpit due to aspartame.

---

[40] *Health Wars by Philip Day*

[41] *Aspartame Consumer Safety Network Fact Sheet*

Frightening isn't it?

Saccharin

350 times sweeter than sugar.

Tested in Canada on rodents in 1977 and found to produce bladder tumours in abnormal quantities in the male. An immediate ban was called but American Congress, pressured by consumer, demand, put it back on the market with a health warning label.

Healthy food to eat

By now you must be wondering what is good to eat.

As mentioned above, eat the way your ancestors used to eat and you body will be reasonably happy. Good food to eat is:

Whole grains

Cook with a little sea salt

Pot barley	Millet
Pearl barley	Oats (whole, flakes, meal)
Brown rice (short, medium)	Rye
Buckwheat (oat groats, noodles [soba]	Wheat (whole, bread, noodles, udon, bulghur)
Corn	Sweet brown rice (mochi)
Quinoa	Couscous

Vegetables
Green / White Vegetables   Stem / Root vegetables

Broccoli	Dandelion Greens	Burdock	Onion
Brussels sprouts	Kale	Carrots	Radish
Bok choy	Leeks	White radish (mooli)	Salsify

Cabbage	Mustard greens	Dandelion roots	Pumpkin
Carrot tops	Parsley		Swede
Cauliflower	Spring onions	Lotus root	Turnip
Chinese cabbage	Turnip greens	Watercress	

SEA SALT Use sparingly.

OILS For use in cooking only.

Unrefined. Sesame, corn. Use sparingly

SOUP   (1 or 2 bowls daily)

Cook with wakame or kombu seaweed and include a variety of vegetables, beans and grains. Change ingredients often.   Season mildly or moderately with:

Mugi (Barley Miso). Genmai (Brown rice) Miso. Hatcho (Soya) Miso. Shoyu (natural Soya sauce).

BEANS AND BEAN PRODUCTS

Cook with wakame or kombu seaweed and season with Shoyu. This should not be more than 10% of the diet if you are suffering from cancer.

FOR REGULAR USE	FOR OCCASIONAL USE	
Aduki	Tofu	Red lentils
Chickpeas	Tempeh	Black eyes

Lentils (green)	Natto	Haricot
Black soybeans	Soya	Seitan
	Split peas	Fu (wheat gluten)
	Kidney	

SEAWEEDS

Good supply of minerals. Only use ¼ inch of Kombu or Arame with your dishes.

Arame	Dulse	Hijiki	Kombu	Irish moss	Wakame

SEEDS AND NUTS

Use as an occasional snack or garnish in cooking. Dry roast and season lightly with sea salt or Shoyu.

SEEDS	NUTS	SPREADS
Pumpkin	Almond	Sesame
Sesame	Chestnut	Peanut butter
Sunflower	Hazelnut	Sunflower
Sesame spread	Peanut	
	Pecan	
	Walnut	

FRUITS DESSERTS

AND GOOD QUALITY SWEETENERS

Apricot	Peaches	Melon	Barley malt	Apple
Raspberry	Raisin	Yinnie syrup	Cherry	Strawberry
Currant	Fruit juice	Pears	Grapes	Sultana
Fruit spreads	Rice syrup			

For proper absorption, fruits should be eaten on their own. They rush to your intestines for digestion in about 30 minutes and will not linger in your stomach. If you eat fruits after your meal, they will fall into your stomach and be jammed with your other food. This will produce acid, fermentation and putrefaction. Not a happy mixture and you may find people talking to you from a distance because of your breath.

You should leave at least 3 hours before a meal and fruits and leave 30 minutes between fruits and your meal.

Kanten: (Natural jelly) Agar agar cooked with fruit.

SEAFOODS

Crab	Bass	Halibut	Sprats	Lobste
Carp	Plaice	Trout	Oyster	Cod
Red snapper	Turbot	Shrimp	Haddock	Sole
Whitefish				

CONDIMENTS

Shoyu	Gomasio	Toasted Nori	Roasted seaweed powder
Takuan	Miso pickles	Umeboshi	Umeboshi paste
Umeboshi vinegar	Tekka	Quick pickles	Home made pickles
Grated ginger	Sauerkraut	Brown rice vinegar	Chopped spring onions

DRINKS

Drink only when thirsty, but drink a comfortable amount.

FOR REGULAR USE	FOR OCCASIONAL USE:
Bancha (twig, three year) tea	Beer
Dandelion coffee	Green tea
Grain coffee	Mineral water
Kombu tea	Sake
Mu tea	
Roasted barley tea	
Roasted rice tea	
Water (well, spring, filtered)	

Thank you for reading this book. I hope you enjoyed it. For more information about my work and the various courses I run, please browse my web site at www.therapies.com

FREE NEWSLETTER

- One in two men and one in three women will get Cancer. Are you safe?
- Did you know that Modern Medicine is the third leading cause of death in our modern society?
- Are there natural products that help Cancer?

If you are interested in different forms of Alternative Therapies and wish to have them explained .. Or wish to learn about natural supplements or products .. Or how to naturally fight off disease and boost your immune system .. Or want facts, data, statistics on the different methods available to help cancers, diabetes, heart problems etc.. Please join my FREE Newsletter at: http://www.therapies.com/ or send a blank email to: newsletter@therapies.par32.com

Other Books by Patrick

May be found at **http://www.therapies.com/ebooks**

Courses/ Lectures and Presentations

Should you be interested in organising one of my courses (see http://www.therapies.com/) at your home/ business premises, please contact me at patrick@therapies.com, I would be delighted to come and teach for you and offer you your course free of charge

About the author

An introduction Patrick Hamouy

http://www.therapies.com/

Patrick Hamouy started his career in computers when he was the founder and owner of a software house. The deep recession that struck the UK in 1991 saw an end to his business that specialised in "Recruitment Packages for Employment Agencies". In a recession, recruitment is at its lowest. His company just took a very quick and impressive nose dive.

This was wonderful as after many years of stress, Patrick's health was very poor. He had serious problems with his liver (like most French men) and was diagnosed as being in a pre-cancerous condition by a Macrobiotic consultant. His large intestines were also a problem and he was suffering from arthritis in his left knee. For many years, Patrick had tried to take care of his health by using natural remedies and he had a fascination for Alternative Therapies.

At last the recession gave him the time to study, as there was no customer in sight from his computer business. He first studied Bach Remedies and having run out of books to read on the subject, he moved on to Aromatherapy.

He joined various evening courses and eventually studied with Raworth College in Dorking. In 1991 he qualified in Anatomy & Physiology and Massage. He then pursued his studies in Aromatherapy and Reflexology and qualified in both. He taught all these therapies to ITEC qualifying standards between 1993 and 2002.

His health improved but his liver was still cause for great concern. In July 1991 he became Macrobiotic and started to eat and live a much healthier life. His two and half years of Macrobiotic studies allowed him to study the effects of different food on the body, the effects of chemicals, and the causes of disease. He followed courses in Oriental

Diagnosis, Cooking, Energetics of food, Shiatsu, Feng Shui, Nine star KI etc..

Patrick started studying various methods of healing in February 1993. Starting with Reiki and then progressing to Seichem and Karuna. Patrick now is a Master is all 3 methods of healing.

Patrick is a qualified Fire Walking Instructor. He studied with Peggy Dylan and her company "Sundoor". Peggy is the originator of the Fire Walking movement in the West.

In December 2000, he started learning EFT (Emotional Freedom Therapy). He now offers courses in this therapy to would be practitioners. Emotional Freedom Therapy is used to get rid of negative emotions quickly and efficiently; a very desirable tool as negative emotions are one of the leading causes of disease.

Nowadays, Patrick teaches Macrobiotics, Oriental Diagnosis, Psychic Development, Emotional Freedom Therapy, Indian Head Massage, Reiki and Karuna healing at his school. He also offers courses in Anatomy & Physiology and Massage through the Internet.

He has authored 4 videos and 4 DVDs in Body massage, Reflexology, Indian Head Massage and Acupressure/On Site massage. He also offers CDs in Reiki meditation to meet your guide, Reiki music with a bell every 3 minutes and Reiki with instructions every 3 minutes. All these are available at www.therapies.com/acatalog

Patrick also gives Macrobiotic consultations to people with poor health. His belief is that in order to eradicate a disease, you must go back to its cause to suppress it. He has studied Metabolic therapies and the use of B17 (Laetrile / Amygdalin), Essiac tea, Hawaiian Noni Juice and Hoxsey remedies to further help his client.

He publishes a regular Newsletter on the Internet (free of charge - see www.therapies.com) The aim of the Newsletter is to help people who have been diagnosed with some disease and do not know who to turn to or what to do. The Newsletter details Patrick's natural approach with Cancer and other serious health conditions.

Since 1997, Patrick has been working with Filipino Bare Hand Surgeons. He takes frequent trips to the Philippines with groups of people who believe their health can be improved by this form of healing (see www.therapies.com/surgery)

He started using enemas on a regular basis end of year 2000.

His health problems are now kept in check through Macrobiotic living and regular Alternative Therapy treatments.

INDEX